The BARKtender's GUIDE
to DOGTAILS and PUPCAKES

Boo zeHound and Elizabeth Dodwell

The BARKtender's Guide™
to Dogtails and Pupcakes
by Boo zeHound and Elizabeth Dodwell

The BARKtender's Guide™
Copyright Elizabeth Dodwell 2012
ISBN 978-0-9853527-4-5

Published by The BARKtender's Guide, LLC
www.BARKtendersGuide.com
www.facebook.com/TheBARKtendersGuide
twitter: @The_BARKtender

Book cover design by Danijela Mijailović
Photos by Scott Bedenbaugh of Pix2Go Studios, Pix2Go.com and stock photos
Page 3 photo courtesy of Southern Hope Humane Society and www.dontgetadog.com
Cover Image Copyright Roman Sotola, steamroller_blues, April Turner, oznuroz, thepiwko, Ruth Black, 2012. Used under license from Shutterstock.com
Pupcake decoration and original designs by Sweets on the Square, Lawrenceville, Georgia. Other designs from the book, Hello, Cupcake!

"It's just a dog."

Some of the cruelest words ever spoken.

To Angel,
who suffered the most deliberate and
contemptuous cruelty at the hands of man, yet
now greets every person as if they are the
most wonderful she has ever known.

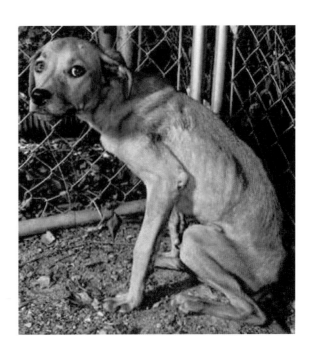

People who say money can't buy happiness have never paid an adoption fee

Angel now

Grrreetings!

The first thing you should know is that a portion of the price you paid for *The BARKtender's Guide* is going to help rescue pets.

Angel, Vinny and Coco, with whom my husband and I share our lives, all came to us from Southern Hope Humane Society in Georgia (southernhopehumane.com). Earning the trio's trust and love has been a truly humbling journey and we are constantly amazed at our canines' capacity for forgiveness.

Food has been an integral part in our pups' transformation. Let's face it, it's one of the most fundamental ways in which we connect with our dogs. Not only do we provide them with daily sustenance, but we offer food to assist in training, as a reward for good behavior and because it helps reinforce the special bond between us.

Researching and testing the BARKtender recipes has been a definite family affair. Somehow, as soon as I start gathering ingredients for pupcakes, the dogs know and line up in the kitchen keeping a careful eye on the proceedings. The moment the oven door is opened to remove the baked treats they are a bundle of barely suppressed excitement.

These recipes have all been developed with your pooch's health in mind. You'll find a number of recipes use gluten-free flour; dairy products are low fat; fresh and organic ingredients replace over-processed products. However, it should be stressed that these *are* treats, *not* a substitute for your dog's daily diet.

Much gratitude is owed to several people without whose help *The BARKtender's Guide* would never have made it to publication. Photographer, Scott Bedenbaugh of Pix2Go.com, for the endless hours he patiently spent ensuring the dogtails, pupcakes and The Tasting Team look brilliant in print. Also, for debugging my computer and saving it from the scrap heap, along with my sanity. Suzanne Stevens who owns and operates Sweets on the Square in Lawrenceville, GA, for decorating the pupcakes in The BARKtender's Guide with some amazing original designs and other popular designs. She also makes some of the best cupcakes you've ever tasted. Dr Nancy Churchill of Gwinnett Animal Hospital in Snellville, GA for advice on foods that are safe for dogs and for helping keep my "kids" safe and well all these years. Robin Taylor, owner of Gwinnett Pet Watchers, Lawrenceville, GA for her invaluable friendship, encouragement and eternal optimism and for allowing her dogs to be part of the Tasting Team. And most of all, my husband, Alex Markovich, who makes all things possible.

Elizabeth Dodwell
Author, Speaker, Humorist, Dog maniac

Contents

Pupcakes 59

Put On The Dog 101

Feeding No-Nos 107

The Tasting Team 111

Did you hear about the cowboy who got himself a dachshund? Everyone kept telling him to get a long, little doggie.

The Bare Bones

Broth is a staple for a number of recipes in *The BARKtender's Guide*. It's really nutritious, easy to make and batches of broth can be divided into small amounts and frozen for future use. Boo uses small freezer baggies that he first labels and dates and from which he removes the air before sealing. This is a great way to pack a lot of broth into a small space. (*Hint:* don't place baggies directly on wire racks in the freezer or they'll get stuck. Put them on a flat surface).

Yes, you can find organic stock in the store. However, it will contain onion, salt, pepper and other ingredients that are *ah-ahs* for your pet. Instead, get friendly with your butcher and fishmonger and ask for meaty bones and fish parts that might otherwise be thrown away. So what if you pay a little? Rover will kiss you all over for being such a wonderful pawrent.

Basic Meat Broth

This is a basic recipe for any meat broth (beef, chicken, lamb, turkey, or a combination of meats), that you can safely give to Fido.

What you need:

- 3 - 4 lbs of meaty bones
- cold water

What to do:

- in a large heavy pan cover the bones with cold water by about 2 inches
- bring to a simmer (not a boil) over medium heat, skimming off the scum that rises to the top
- partially cover the pot and continue to slow simmer for 2 - 3 hours
- check occasionally and skim if necessary. If the water level drops below the bones add a little more *hot* water
- when done, strain the broth to remove the meat and bones
- **be sure to discard the bones*** though it's OK to save the meat to give to Bowser
- refrigerate the broth overnight. The fat will rise to the top and solidify
- remove and discard the fat
- the broth should now be gel-like.
- at this stage, you can divide the broth into containers and refrigerate or freeze 'til needed. Or, if you want to remove any traces of remaining fat, bring the broth to room temperature and strain through a coffee filter 'til completely clear, then refrigerate or freeze

*NEVER give your dog cooked bones. They can easily splinter and cause very serious injuries.

Basic Fish Broth

What you need:

- about 3 lbs of any combination of fish spines, heads and tails (do **not** use shellfish)
- 1 gallon cold water

What to do:

- wash tails and heads in cold water and cut out any gills (they tend to be bitter)
- in a large pot add all the fish pieces with the water
- bring to a boil, cover and simmer on low for one hour
- if the water level drops too low, add a little *hot* water
- when done, strain through a fine mesh strainer lined with cheesecloth or a large coffee filter; discard the bones, skin, etc.
- refrigerate or freeze the broth as needed

Basic Vegetable Broth

What you need:

- any combination of "safe" vegetables (see below) but definitely NO **onion**
- cold water

What to do:

- wash the vegetables and chop them roughly (no need to peel anything but cut out any bad parts)
- put them in a heavy pot and cover with water by about two inches
- bring to a slow simmer, cover and leave for about 1 hour, stirring occasionally
- strain through a fine sieve with cheesecloth or a coffee filter
- refrigerate or freeze the broth as needed

Safe vegetables include:

Asparagus - beetroot - broccoli - cabbage - carrots - cauliflower - celery - green beans - kale - parsley - squash - sweet potato.

If in any doubt about an ingredient - check with your vet.

A dog can express more with his tail in minutes than his owner can express with his tongue in hours.

Ta Dah!

Just a note about portion sizes:

Our doggie drink recipes have been created with an average to large size dog in mind. This means you will need to adjust portions for your Toy Yorkie or St Bernard.

Always keep in mind that any time you give your BFF a food that he or she has not had before (or make any change in diet, for that matter) begin with just a small amount and introduce the food gradually. It's a myth that dogs have cast iron stomachs (OK, maybe yours does) and changes in diet can sometimes cause digestive problems.

DOGTAILS

Slow Comfortable Sniff

Dogs have an incredible sense of smell. They have been used to track down everything from drugs, corpses, bombs and bumblebees. Some amazing canines are even able to do duty as early detection devices for illnesses such as lung cancer.

Now you can give Fido's sniffer a reason to wiggle with joy when you make and shake this yummy drink.

What you need:

- 2 tbsp all natural or organic peanut butter (without sugar and little or no salt)
- 1 cup 100% carrot juice*
- 1/3 cup low fat, plain yogurt
- 2 tsp rice syrup
- Carrot sticks for stirrers

What to do:

- add room temperature peanut butter to a cocktail shaker with the rice syrup and blend thoroughly with a spoon
- next add the yogurt and ¼ cup carrot juice and continue to blend 'til the mix is a smooth paste
- pour in the remaining carrot juice and shake the mixture as hard as your dog wags his or her tail
- serve up or over ice as preferred, with a carrot stick in each dogtail

*Make carrot juice without a juicer:

- puree 2 lbs of washed, but not peeled, carrots with a little water in a blender
- add 2 cups of hot water; stir and let steep for 30 minutes
- strain through a fine sieve, refrigerate and use within 24 hours

Other things dogs love to sniff:

- *Sweaty armpits.*
- *Anything that's been dead for at least three days, especially if it's in the middle of the road.*
- *Your mother-in-law's rear end (actually, anybody's will do).*
- *Dirty underwear that's been stuck for months behind the washing machine.*
- *The neighbor's trash (because they're into hot dogs and pizza, not the broccoli and granola you like).*

Dogfather

"Do you have faith in my judgement?

Do I have your loyalty?

I'm gonna make you an offer you won't refuse. Okay? I want you to leave it all to me. Go on, go back to the party and drink, drink. And give me a drop."

~ Dog Corleone

What you need:

- 1 cup pure homemade chicken broth (see page 11)
- 1 tbsp pureed 100% pumpkin (NOT pie filling)
- ½ cup carrot juice* (eg Odwalla, Bolthouse or Virgin Extracts carrot powder)
- ½ cup unflavored Pedialite**

What to do:

- put the pumpkin and carrot juice in a cocktail shaker and dry shake with vigor
- add the chicken broth, Pedialite and 1 cup of ice cubes and shake again
- pour, with the ice, into your pup's favorite dogtail vessel

*See page 17 to make carrot juice without a juicer

**Pedialite is sometimes given as a remedy for dehydration. Dogs don't care for the taste, so if your little mafia mutt needs a liquid boost this tasty mix might be the answer. As always, check with your vet first.

A watchdog is a dog kept to guard your home, usually by sleeping where a burglar would awaken the household by falling over him.

Lappletini

Even puppies can enjoy this type of 'tini. Maybe it will help keep the *dog*ter away.

What you need:

- ¼ cup pure apple juice, no sugar, citric acid or other additives*
- 1 cup homemade turkey broth (see page 11)
- ¼ cup low fat cottage cheese
- ½ cup cracked ice
- apple slice for garnish

What to do:

- add all ingredients to a blender
- blend on high 'til the mix is smooth
- pour into a barktini glass
- garnish with the apple and lap it up

Cocktail umbrellas look fun - just be sure to remove them before giving Molly her drink

*Dogs can drink small quantities of fruit juice but be sure it is free of any additives and artificial colors. Apple juice has a lot of natural sugar and too much can cause diarrhea and other stomach upset in some pets.

Fuzzy Navel

It's great to be a dog because....

If you grow hair in weird places no-one notices

You probably know that the people version of the Fuzzy Navel combines peach and orange. We've given a nod to that by including a little fresh peach in the doggy drink and, combined with the carrot, that adds enough sweetness to keep your pup very happy.

What you need:

- 1 cup pure homemade beef broth (see page 11)
- ¼ cup chopped carrot
- ¼ cup chopped, peeled peach (no pits - they contain a little cyanide)
- ¼ tsp spirulina powder* (optional)
- ½ tsp bone meal powder (optional)
- 1 cup cracked ice
- carrot stick or fresh peach for garnish

- add all ingredients to a blender
- blend to a slushy consistency
- pour into a suitable bowl
- serve with the carrot stick stirrer or slice of peach

*Spirulina is believed to help strengthen the immune system

A Shaggy Dog Story:

The "shaggy dog story" is a long-winded yarn that holds the listeners in expectation of a funny climax but ends in disappointment. It's also come to mean a joke that ends with a punch line that's recognizable as a familiar saying. Like this:

In a small local bar the owner's little dog was a favorite with the patrons, so they were very upset when the mutt died.

Everyone met to discuss how they could remember the little guy and the decision was made to cut off his tail and hang it behind the bar to remind them how his tail would wag furiously in greeting.

Meanwhile, the dog went up to heaven and was about to run through the pearly gates when he was stopped by Saint Peter, who asked where the pup thought he was going.

"I've been a good dog, so I'm going into Heaven where I belong."

"I'm sorry," replied Saint Peter, "but Heaven is a place of perfection and I see you don't have your tail. Without it, you can't come in."

The little dog explained what had happened back on earth. Saint Peter told him to go back down and retrieve his tail.

"But it's the middle of the night," protested the tailless pooch. "The bar will be closed!"

Saint Peter would not change his mind and so the dog returned to earth where he scratched on the door of the bar 'til the bartender (who lived upstairs) came down and opened it.

"My goodness, it's the spirit of the little dog. What can I do for you?" asked the bartender.

The dog related how he wasn't allowed into heaven without his tail and needed it back.

"I'd really love to help you," the bartender replied, "but my liquor license doesn't allow me to retail spirits after hours."

Bone-ito

Salud! to the Bonito, a refreshing libation on a hot summer's day. And this recipe is for sharing, so get close to a few friends. With the fresh mint in this recipe you won't have to worry about dog breath.

What you need:

- ½ a small, seedless watermelon (seeds can cause an upset tummy)
- 2 tbsp all natural peanut butter (with no sugar and no salt)
- 1 cup low fat, plain yogurt
- 2 tsp rice syrup
- ¼ cup fresh mint leaves, loosely packed

What to do:

- scoop the fruit from the watermelon and roughly chop
- blend all the ingredients together
- serve over ice in individual dishes or use the empty watermelon half as a punch bowl

Three male dogs set eyes on a beautiful female poodle. Aware of her charms, Fifi said, "I will go out with the first one of you who can use the words 'liver' and 'cheese' together in an intelligent sentence."

Immediately the Lab said, "I like liver and cheese."

"No imagination at all," said Fifi.

Next was the hunky Rottweiler, who blurted, "I hate liver and cheese."

"That's worse than the Lab," Fifi replied.

Last, a tiny chihuahua smiled at his opponents, gave the poodle a knowing wink, and said, "Liver alone, cheese mine."

"Nurse. Quick!
I need an IV drip of
Hair of the Dog."

Hair of the Dog

Adding raw egg to a hangover recipe is an age old cure. While Rex should never need that kind of help (because you would never be foolish enough to give him alcohol) we have added egg to our Hair of the Dog dogtail.

The egg is a great source of nutrients and amino acids, though there are some concerns that eggs may contain salmonella. So choose very fresh, organic products or omit the egg from the recipe if you have doubts. Rex will still enjoy his drink.

What you need:

- 2 cups turkey broth (recipe on page 11)
- 1 organic fresh egg
- ½ cup 100% pure pumpkin (NOT pie filling)
- 1 tbsp blackstrap molasses
- cinnamon powder* for garnish

What to do:

- put all the ingredients in a blender and run on a low setting 'til just mixed
- serve over ice with just one small shake of cinnamon

*Cinnamon purportedly has antifungal, antibacterial and antimicrobial properties and most dogs seem to like the taste. So a little dash will do it!

- In a veterinarian's waiting room: "Be back in 5 minutes. Sit Stay"

- Puppies work better than Prozac

- If your dog is fat, you aren't getting enough exercise

Pina Doglada

Is this what people mean by "It's a dog's life?"

What you need:

- ½ cup chicken broth (see page 11)
- ¼ cup 100% pure pineapple juice
- ½ cup sugar free, low fat plain yogurt
- 1 tbsp flax seed oil
- 2 tsp rice syrup
- 1 cup cracked ice
- pineapple (unsweetened) piece* for garnish

What to do:

- add all ingredients except the pineapple piece to a blender
- run on high 'til texture is slushy
- pour into a "dogtail" bowl
- garnish with the pineapple

*Fresh is best but canned with no added sugar is OK.

If you happen to have a fresh coconut around, you could tap into it for a little water to add to this dogtail. Just a splash will do to make an even better copy of the pet person's Pina Colada. Just be sure to avoid commercial coconut waters that have sugar and other additives.

Hint: Frozen pineapple can be a fun treat for your dog, and though it has a lot of natural sugar, it also contains calcium and potassium.

Doghattan

Sophisticated yet simple. The Doghattan is a canine classic, served muttini style.

What you need:

- ½ cup beef broth (recipe on page 11)
- ½ cup chicken broth
- ½ cup vegetable broth (recipe on page 12)
- Pinch of bone meal powder (see note on page 110)
- Small sprig of fresh parsley

What to do:

- add the liquid ingredients to an ice-filled cocktail shaker
- shake like a wet dog and strain into your mutt's favorite dish
- sprinkle a little bone meal powder on top
- lay the parsley in the center of the dish

Ah, city life: Doggy day care, fire hydrants, apartment dwelling and..... cocktail bars.

Sadly, the canine presence is now pooh-poohed in eateries and drinking establishments. But smart pooches aren't licked. They know they can enjoy a Dogtail or two with a few friends in the comfort of their own home.

"Waiter, there's a kitten in my drink."

"Is it Yappy Hour yet?"

Barkardi Cocktail

What you need:

- 1 cup homemade salmon broth (recipe on page 12)
- ¼ cup organic sugar-free apple juice (see notes on page 21)
- ¼ cup cooked sweet potato
- 2 fresh mint leaves, torn
- 1 extra mint leaf for garnish

What to do:

- puree the sweet potato with a little of the salmon broth in a blender
- put the sweet potato puree in a cocktail shaker with the remaining salmon broth, apple juice and torn mint leaves and 8 cubes of ice
- shake well then pour into your dog's dish with the ice
- top with a single mint leaf

"I'm barking mad for a Barkardi Cocktail"

Barking dogs seldom bite.
Scratch that! It depends if they're barking for one of their favorite doggy cocktails.

Angel's Kiss

What you need:

- ½ cup plain low-fat yogurt
- ¼ tsp alcohol-free vanilla (you can make your own; recipe on page 65)
- 1 tsp 100% pure peanut butter, room temperature
- ½ tsp carob powder
- 1 tsp rice syrup
- 1 large ripe strawberry

What to do:

- combine all the ingredients in a cocktail shaker and dry shake very vigorously
- add a few ice cubes and shake again 'til your hands begin to freeze
- pour into your favorite barktini bowl
- slit the strawberry and hang it on the side of the bowl for garnish

"Let me give you a real Angel kiss. Know what I mean?"

Frozen Doguiri

Papaya is not always easy to find and it's something of an acquired taste for most pups. But this recipe will work just as well with mango, peach or apricot. Be sure to use fresh fruit and keep in mind that if your pet has never had these fruits before, give just a small portion. And always keep the pits away from Duke and Duchess. Not only are they a choking hazard but they contain a little cyanide.

What you need:

- 1 cup chicken broth (recipe on page 11)
- ½ cup pork broth (meat broth recipe on page 11)
- ¼ cup chopped fresh papaya or mango
- 1 tsp rice syrup
- Bacon bits for garnish or all meat hot dog* (optional)

What to do:

- put all the ingredients, except bacon bits, in a blender with ice
- blend on high 'til slushy in texture
- pour into bowls and sprinkle bacon bits on top on use the hot dog as a stirrer

Note: If your dog is like Angel, Vinny and Coco, turning their noses up at icy drinks, you can make a Doguiri by pureeing the fruit with a tbsp of water and then dry shaking (without ice) the ingredients 'til well mixed.

So there's a wiener in this drink. The BARKtender took some artistic license but doesn't recommend hot dogs or sausages for your BFF because of the salt, sugar and nitrite content.

Read notes on page 108 for more information on foods that are safe for dogs.

"One has to be prepared for these icy drinks"

Frisky Sour

What you need:

- 2 cans of no-salt tuna in water*
- Decaffeinated green tea (mild brew)**

What to do:

- strain the liquid from the cans of tuna and set the meat aside to make tuna salad (or casserole) for yourself
- pour the tuna liquid over ice with an equal amount of decaf green tea and stir
- serve with a carrot stick stirrer or cucumber rose

*Your local health food store will carry no-salt tuna, or there is a wide selection online.
**Green tea can cause minor tummy upset in some dogs

Nowadays, paralysis is not synonymous with euthanasia. A doggy wheelchair can enable many mutts to continue living a full and frisky life. With rehabilitation some dogs may even regain use of their limbs. No matter what, keep giving Rex lots of love, love, love... and the occasional Frisky Sour.

Note:
There are several companies that offer canine carts and it's even possible to get rear and quad carts (they are towable). The BARKtender urges you to do careful research before buying. Some wheelchairs tend to put more pressure on the soft tissue and cause painful chafing. And if your pet has progressive disabilities, look for a wheelchair that is upgradable to meet Lassie's continuing needs.
Our photographer, Scott Bedenbaugh, has also designed an amazing 'Wobble Board' that helps challenge a dog's core musculature. Find out more at CanineRehabSystems.com.

For some, mobility is the gift of life

Young Jack was practicing the violin in the living room while his father was trying to read in the den. The family dog was lying in the den, and as the screeching sounds of Jack's violin reached the dog's ears, he began to howl loudly.

The father listened to the dog and the violin as long as he could. Then he jumped up, slammed his paper to the floor and yelled above the noise, "For Pete's sake, can't you play something the dog doesn't know?!"

Howling Banana Banshee

If your pup doesn't like icy cold drinks, you can still make this dogtail in the blender and just omit the ice.

What you need:

- ½ cup mild brewed chamomile tea*
- ½ cup plain low fat yogurt
- ½ a small banana, diced
- 1 tbsp 100% pure peanut butter, unsweetened
- 1 tbsp rice syrup

What to do:

- combine all ingredients in a blender with 8 - 10 ice cubes
- run on high 'til smooth
- serve with a small slice of banana for garnish

"It's Yappy Hooooouuuurr"

Chamomile is considered to have many of the same properties for dogs as for their guardians. However, some pooches are allergic to it, so always check for sensitivity before giving the herb, especially if your pet is already prone to hay fever or other plant allergies.

Dogmopolitan

The cosmopolitan dog is happy to consort cheek by jowl with canines of all breeds and sizes and his choice of dogtail reflects his easy approach to life.

What you need:

- ½ cup turkey broth (recipe on page 11)
- ½ cup pork broth (meat broth recipe on page 11)
- 1 tbsp low fat cream cheese or neufchatel, room temperature
- cucumber for garnish

Note: See page 103 for instructions on how to make a cucumber spiral

What to do:

- add the cream cheese to a cocktail shaker with 2 tbsp of broth
- using a spoon, blend the cheese into the broth
- add the remaining broth and dry shake thoroughly
- add a few ice cubes and shake again
- pour with the ice into a bowl
- garnish with the cucumber

"I'm so happy, happy, happy! I see a Pink Poodle in my future."

Pink Poodle

What you need:

- ½ cup low fat cottage cheese
- ½ cup fresh ripe strawberries, chopped*
- ¼ cup beet juice**
- ¼ cup purified water
- 1 tsp rice syrup
- Strawberry and rawhide strip for garnish

What to do:

- prepare a strawberry rose garnish according to instructions on page 103
- puree the cottage cheese and strawberries together
- put all ingredients in a shaker and dry shake (without ice)
- serve over ice and add the "rose"

*Apparently, strawberries have an enzyme in them that'll help keep your dog's teeth white.

**If you can't juice your own, there are a number of juices and powders on the market, including Smart Basics, Dynamic Health and Biotta.

"If you pick up a starving dog and make him prosperous, he will not bite you. This is the principal difference between a dog and a man."
--Mark Twain

Will give
kisses for
healthy
food

Perfect Good Boy

What you need:

- 1 cup fish broth (see page 11)
- 1 cup pork broth (recipe on page 11)
- 1 organic raw egg (see notes on page 110)
- 1 tsp bone meal (human consumption grade)

What to do:

- add all ingredients to a cocktail shaker half-filled with ice
- shake with as much energy as your dog digs for a bone
- strain the contents into bowls; there should be a nice froth on top
- garnish with a simple parsley sprig

From a dog's perspective, when it comes to training, jerk is a noun, not a verb

"My skin isn't wrinkled,
it's just relaxed fit."

Dirty Muttini

This is where it began. Vinny was about to enjoy a bowl of chicken broth. We decided to put some in a martini glass, add a chicken jerky stirrer, sit Mr. V at the bar with it and take a picture. Soon people were asking about the "Dirty Muttini" and so the idea for The BARKtender's Guide was born.

What you need:

- ½ cup chicken broth (see page 11 for recipe)
- ½ cup filtered or spring water
- Small chicken jerky strip*

What to do:

- add the broth and water to ice in a mixing tin
- stir then strain into a muttini bowl (that's your dog's favorite dish)
- garnish with the jerky

A dog with a bandage on one leg limped into a saloon in the Wild West and announced, "I'm looking for the man that shot my paw."

High Ball

What you need:

- 1 cup pork broth (see recipe on page 11)
- ¼ cup organic sugar free apple juice*
- 1 tsp rice syrup
- Sam's Yams Bichon Fries Sweet Potato chew for garnish, or a slice of apple

What to do:

- add the broth, apple juice and syrup to a mixing tin
- stir well to blend the syrup into the liquid
- pour over ice in bowls
- use the Bichon Fries chew as a "stirrer"

Did you know...?

The 1937 Agatha Christie mystery, "Dumb Witness," was originally intended to be called, "Incident of the Dog's Ball."

The novel features Bob, a ball-loving wire-haired terrier and cerebral super-sleuth, Hercule Poirot. The book is dedicated to Christie's own wire-haired terrier, Peter; "A dog in a thousand".

*Juice your own or try a product like Simply Apple or Odwalla All Natural

Dogs chasing balls are like people eating potato chips - you
can't stop at one

"Of course it's a toy — and it's mine!"

Mai Toy

What you need:

- 1 cup frozen chopped seedless watermelon
- ½ cup low fat plain yogurt
- ¼ cup pure pumpkin (NOT pie filling)
- 1 tsp carob powder
- 1 tsp rice syrup (optional)
- watermelon slices or blueberry stick for garnish

What to do:

- put all the ingredients in a blender, except the garnish
- add 6 - 8 ice cubes and blend 'til slushy
- pour into dogtail dishes (Fido's fave bowl)
- for the blueberry stick, thread fresh berries on a rawhide strip

Sex in the Dog Park

What you need:

- 1 cup of vegetable broth (recipe on page 12)
- 1 cup chicken liver water, recipe below
- ¼ cup low fat cottage cheese
- ¼ cup chopped cooked sweet potato (with skin on)
- chicken liver for garnish

What to do:

For the chicken livers:

- cover chicken livers with water in a saucepan and bring to a boil. Boil for 5 minutes
- remove the livers (keep the water) and refrigerate immediately. Let the water cool for a while before refrigerating

For the dogtail:

- add the vegetable broth, chicken liver water, cottage cheese and sweet potato to a blender
- run on high 'til the mix is smooth
- pour over ice in bowls and garnish with a cooked chicken liver (or just a slice for smaller pups)

Everybody who has a dog calls him "Rover" or "Boy". I call my dog "Sex".

Now, Sex has been very embarrassing to me. When I went to get his license, I told the clerk I would like to have a license for Sex. He said, "I'd like to have one too." Then I said, "But this is a dog." He said "I don't care what she looks like." Then I said, "You don't understand, I've had Sex since I was 9 year's old." He said I must have been quite a kid.

When I got married and went on my honeymoon, I took the dog with me. I told the hotel clerk that I wanted a room for my wife and me and a special room for Sex. He said that every room in the place was for sex. I said, "You don't understand, Sex keeps me awake at night." The Clerk said, "Me too."

Last night Sex ran off. I spent hours looking around town for him. A cop came over to me and asked, "What are you doing in this alley at 4 in the morning?" I said, "I'm looking for Sex..."

My case comes up on Friday...

♪♪ I ain't nothin' but a bad hound,
Though I'm crazy over you. ♪ ♪♪

Let me slobber on your ear lobe
And I promise you will drool. ♫ ♫

Every dog has his day

Freddy Mudchucker

What you need:

- 1 cup chicken broth (recipe on page 11)
- 1 cup beef broth (see page 11)
- 1 cup fish broth (see page 12)
- 1 very fresh organic raw egg
- 1 tsp spirulina powder
- splash of beetroot juice*
- frozen carrot juice bone for garnish

What to do:

- to make the frozen carrot bones, mix equal parts carrot juice and water then pour into your mold
- blend broth, eggs, spirulina and beet juice in a blender, or whisk well in a bowl
- the egg will give the drink a lovely froth
- pour over ice
- add the frozen carrot juice bone or a fresh carrot stick

If you can't juice your own, there are a number of juices and powders on the market, including Smart Basics, Dynamic Health and Biotta.

"Give me pupcakes,
            or the slipper goes"

Pupcakes

No creature is more generous with love than a puppy

Droolin' On a Sunday Afternoon

What you need:

- 1 cup whole wheat flour
- 1 tsp baking soda
- ¼ cup 100% pure peanut butter, no sugar or additives
- ¼ cup vegetable oil
- 1 egg
- ½ cup pureed carrot (or you can use baby food carrot)
- ½ cup shredded fresh carrot
- 1 tsp non-alcoholic vanilla*
- 2 tbsp rice syrup

The BARKtender suggests cream cheese frosting for these pupcakes (recipe on page 104)

What to do:

- preheat oven to 350 F and put baking cups in a muffin pan
- whisk together the flour and baking soda
- create a "well" in the center of the flour mix and drop in the remaining ingredients; mix thoroughly with the whisk
- fill the baking cups about ¾ full with the mixture
- bake for about 18-20 minutes or until a toothpick inserted into the pupcakes comes out clean
- let sit for 2 or 3 minutes then remove the pupcakes to a cooling rack
- allow to cool completely before frosting
- refrigerate or freeze if not using immediately

Yields 12 standard pupcakes
or about 25 minis

*Make your own vanilla extract
with our recipe on page 65*

Give a Dog a Bone

What you need:

- 1 ¾ cups gluten-free, multi-purpose flour
- 1 tsp baking soda
- 1 tsp baking powder
- 1 cup low-fat cottage cheese
- 2 jars (2.5 oz size) turkey baby food, or you can puree fresh turkey meat with a little water
- 2 eggs
- 2 tbs black molasses
- 1 tbsp vegetable oil
- 1 tbsp flax seed oil*
- 2 tsp bone meal

What to do:

- preheat oven to 350 F and line a muffin pan with baking cups
- whisk together all the dry ingredients
- create a well in the center of the flour mix and add all other ingredients
- combine everything with the whisk or wooden spoon 'til well blended
- spoon the batter into the cups to about ¾ full
- bake for 18- 20 minutes or until a toothpick inserted in a pupcake comes out clean
- cool in the pan for a few minutes, then move to a cooling rack
- before serving push a chew treat in the middle; we like Merrick Flossies

*OK to use just veg oil

Yields 12 - 15 pupcakes, or about 25 minis

The FDA lists 10 reasons why you should never give Fido a bone. Raw diet proponents generally insist they are fine. The BARKtender's Guide urges that you do your own due diligence but is adamant that cooked bones are NEVER safe. Raw bones, though softer and more easily digestible, still have the potential to cause a number of problems from broken teeth to dangerous obstructions, constipation and peritonitis.
So why not just give Fido a pupcake?

"Please, sir.
I want some more."

Pawty Animal Pupcakes

What you need:

- 1 cup gluten-free, all-purpose flour (eg. King Arthur or Bob's Red Mill)
- ¼ cup rolled oats
- 1 tsp baking powder
- ½ tsp baking soda
- ½ tsp cinnamon
- ¼ cup organic plain (unsweetened) low-fat yogurt
- ¼ cup vegetable oil
- 1 cup chopped **seedless** watermelon (don't drain)
- 1 tsp alcohol-free vanilla (readily available online and at many local health food stores or make your own with the recipe on the next page)
- 2 tbsp rice syrup
- 1 egg

What to do:

- preheat oven to 350 F
- put mini baking cups in a muffin pan
- blend all the dry ingredients in a large bowl with a hand whisk
- make a well in the flour mix and add the yogurt, oil, vanilla, rice syrup and egg
- whisk together, gradually incorporating the dry ingredients
- with a spoon or spatula, blend in the watermelon
- if the mix is too moist, add a little more flour
- spoon into the baking cups
- bake for 10 - 12 minutes. Pupcakes are done when a toothpick inserted in the middle comes out clean
- move to a cooling rack
- frost with a plain cream cheese frosting (recipe on page 104)
- sprinkle just a tiny bit of cinnamon powder on top

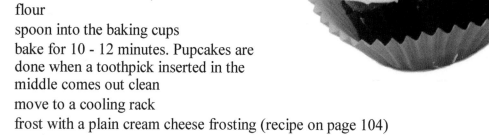

Yields 20 - 25 mini pupcakes

Vanilla Extract

What you need:

- 2 vanilla beans
- 12 oz food grade glycerin*
- 4 oz warm water

What to do:

- mix the glycerin and warm water in a glass jar
- slit beans down the middle to expose the seeds and add to the liquid
- seal, shake and set in a dark place (or use a dark jar)
- shake every few days
- your vanilla extract will be ready in 1 month

*Glycerine is a natural product typically obtained from palm and vegetable oils. It is an alternative to alcohol for preserving herbal tinctures.

Party like an animal, sleep like a dog.

"Red Rover, Red Rover,
send a pupcake right over"

Red Rover Pupcakes

What you need:

- 1 ½ cups gluten-free flour
- ½ cup rolled oats
- 2 tsp baking powder
- ½ tsp baking soda
- ½ cup pureed 100% pure pumpkin (NOT pie filling)
- ¼ cup unsweetened, pure beetroot juice (eg. Smart Basics, Dynamic Health and Biotta)
- ¼ cup vegetable oil
- 2 tbsp rice syrup
- 2 eggs
- 1 small cooked sweet potato, chopped, skin on
- 1 cup grated cheddar cheese
- water, if necessary

What to do:

- preheat the oven to 400 F
- line muffin pans with baking cups
- whisk together the dry ingredients in a large bowl
- make a "well" in the center and add the pumpkin, beet juice, oil, syrup and eggs
- combine wet and dry ingredients so 'til they're well blended
- if the mix is a little dry, add in a tablespoon or two of water
- stir in the sweet potato and cheese
- fill the baking cups with the mixture
- bake for about 15 minutes (10 minutes for mini pupcakes) or 'til a toothpick inserted in a pupcake comes out clean
- cool for a few minutes in the pan then move to a cooling rack
- let cool before frosting

Yields about 15 regular pupcakes or 30 minis

Note: To frost the pupcake shown, use cream cheese frosting colored with carob.

Woof It Down

What you need:

- 1 ½ cups whole wheat flour
- ¼ cup oatmeal flour
- 2 tsps baking powder
- ½ tsp baking soda
- 1 lg apple
- ½ cup water
- ½ cup plain low fat yogurt
- ¼ cup vegetable oil
- 2 eggs
- 2 tbsp rice syrup
- 1 cup grated cheddar

What to do:

- preheat oven to 400 F and line muffin tins with baking cups
- core and dice the apple and puree with the water then set aside
- in a bowl, whisk together the dry ingredients (flour, oatmeal, baking powder, baking soda)
- make a well in the flour mix and add the yogurt, oil, rice syrup, eggs and apple puree
- with the whisk, blend wet and dry ingredients together
- when thoroughly blended, add the cheese and mix with a spoon
- fill the baking cups about ¾ full with the mixture
- bake for about 20 minutes or until a toothpick inserted in the center of a pupcake comes out clean
- let the muffins rest for a while, then remove from the pan and cool on a wire rack
- finish with peanut butter frosting (recipe on page 104)

Note: Always remember to remove the paper baking cup before giving Bella her treat

Yields 16 - 18 standard size pupcakes

Macho Mutt

What you need:

- 1 cup oat flour*
- ½ cup brown rice flour*
- ½ cup rolled oats
- 1 tsp oat bran
- 2 tsp baking powder
- ½ tsp baking soda
- 4 oz beef liver
- ½ cup pork broth (recipe on page 11)
- ¼ cup vegetable oil
- 2 eggs
- 1 tbsp molasses
- ½ cup mashed potato
- extra tbsp or two of water, if needed

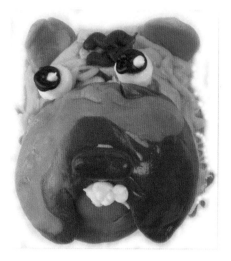

What to do:

- preheat the oven to 350 F
- prepare a muffin pan by lining with baking cups
- roughly chop the liver and puree with the pork broth then set aside
- put all the dry ingredients in a large bowl and whisk them together thoroughly
- to the liver puree, add all the other ingredients except the water and blend well
- a little at a time add the dry ingredients to the wet, adding a little water if needed, so you have a stiff batter
- fill the baking cups with the batter and bake for 20 - 22 minutes or until a toothpick inserted in the middle of a pupcake comes out clean
- after 2 or 3 minutes move the pupcakes to a wire rack to cool

Yields about 1 dozen pupcakes

*Oat and rice flour are often gluten-free but, if you need to be sure it is safe for your sensitive pup, the packaging should read "Certified gluten-free."

Note: you can frost your Macho Mutt using cream cheese and peanut butter frostings colored with carob powder.

Real dogs eat pupcakes
....and they like little puppies

Pound Pupcake

What you need:

- 1 cup gluten-free flour (eg. King Arthur or Bob's Red Mill)
- ½ tsp baking powder
- ½ tsp baking soda
- ½ cup carrots and peas pureed with a ¼ cup water (or use baby food)
- 1 jar (2.5 oz) baby food chicken, or fresh chicken pureed with a little water
- 1 tsp organic tomato paste
- 1 tbsp dried parsley flakes or 2 tbsp chopped fresh parsley
- 1 raw egg
- 1 cooked egg, chopped small
- 1 cooked egg, sliced

What to do:

- preheat the oven to 350 F
- add baking cups to a muffin pan
- whisk the flour, baking powder and baking soda together in a large bowl
- make a "well" in the middle of the dry mix and add all the other ingredients except the chopped egg
- blend the wet and dry ingredients together with a wooden spoon
- when thoroughly mixed, stir in the cooked chopped egg
- drop the mix into standard baking cups
- bake for 15 - 18 minutes, 'til a toothpick comes out clean from the center of a pupcake
- cool in the pan for 2 or 3 minutes then move the pupcakes to a wire rack
- instead of frosting, place a slice of cooked egg on top of each pupcake and add a tiny sprig of parsley

Yields 6 pupcakes

According to the Humane Society of the United States, four million cats and dogs—about one every eight seconds—are put down in U.S. shelters each year.

Why not give a dog a home... and a pupcake, of course.

He is your friend, your partner, your defender, your dog. You are his life, his love, his leader. He will be yours, faithful and true, to the last beat of his heart. You owe it to him to be worthy of such devotion.

My dog was growling at everyone the other day.
Still, what can you expect from a cross-breed?

Dog Day Afternoon

In a dog eat pupcake world, the consequences are sublime

What you need:

- 4 cups dry dog food*
- 1 cup wet dog food*
- 1 cup mashed sweet potato
- 1 cup mashed ripe banana
- 1/3 cup rice syrup
- 1/3 cup canola oil
- 1 apple, finely chopped

*Your pup's favorite quality brand

What to do:

- pre-heat oven to 350 F
- thoroughly mix all ingredients except the apple. If the mix seems too dry, add a little water
- stir in the apple
- fill baking cups set in muffin tins
- cook for 15 - 20 minutes or 'til a toothpick inserted in the middle comes out clean
- let the pupcakes sit for a few minutes, then move to a wire rack to cool
- no frosting needed. These may not look great to you but Lulu will love them

Yields 10 - 12 pupcakes

Petit Paws

What you need:

- 1 cup whole wheat flour
- 1 tsp baking soda
- 1 heaping tsp carob powder
- ½ cup low fat plain yogurt
- ½ cup 100 % pure pumkpin (NOT pie filling)
- 1 egg
- 2 tbsp vegetable oil
- 2 tbsp molasses
- ½ tsp non-alcoholic vanilla*
- water, if necessary

What to do:

- preheat the oven to 350 F
- line a muffin pan with baking cups
- put all the dry ingredients in a large bowl and whisk them together
- create a well in the middle of the dry mix and add the yogurt, egg, oil, molasses, pumpkin and vanilla
- beat the wet ingredients together and gradually incorporate the dry mix into the batter, adding a little water if the batter seems too stiff.
- fill the baking cups and bake for about 20 minutes for standard size or 12 minutes for mini pupcakes. The pupcakes are done when a toothpick inserted into their middle comes out clean
- remove from the oven and let sit in the muffin pan for 3 or 4 minutes then place on a cooling rack

Yields about 24 mini pupcakes and 10 standard size

You can make your own vanilla extract using the recipe on page 65

Note: Directions for creating the "lollipup" are on page 105

Tres Licks Pupcakes

What you need:

- 1 cup whole wheat flour
- 1 tsp baking powder
- ¼ tsp baking soda
- ¼ cup plain low-fat yogurt
- 2 ½ tbsp vegetable oil
- 2 tbsp molasses
- 1 lg egg
- ¼ cup fine chopped apple
- ¼ cup grated carrot
- ½ cup grated cheddar cheese

What to do:

- preheat the oven to 350 F and prep a muffin pan by lining it with baking cups
- in a large bowl, stir together the dry ingredients
- add the yogurt, oil, molasses and egg
- blend all the ingredients together thoroughly
- gradually stir in the apple, carrot and ¼ cup of cheese
- drop the mixture into the baking cups
- bake for 15 minutes then remove and quickly sprinkle the remaining ¼ cup of grated cheddar on top of each pupcake

- return to the oven for another 5 minutes or until a toothpick inserted in the middle of a pupcake comes out clean
- let sit for 2 or 3 minutes then move to a cooling rack

Yields 10 pupcakes

There are several reasons why your dog might lick you:

1. *Affection, of course*
2. *It could be a submissive gesture*
3. *Your dog might like the taste of salty skin*

Say, "Cheesey pupcakes."

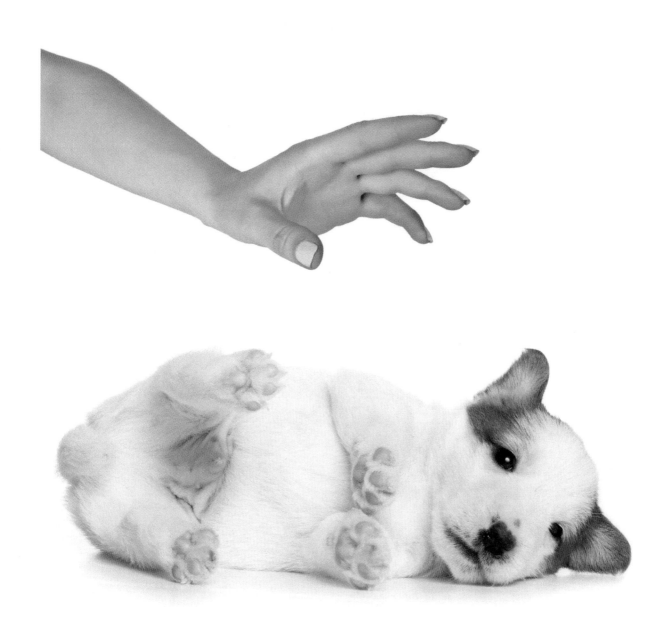

"Ready when you are!"

Well Tickle My Tummy

What you need:

- 1 cup oat flour

- ¾ cup tapioca flour
- ½ cup rolled oats
- 2 tsp baking powder
- ½ tsp baking soda
- ½ cup cooked, flaked salmon*
- 1 - 2 tbsp of the salmon water
- ¼ cup vegetable oil
- 2 eggs
- 1 cup grated cheddar cheese
- ½ cup chopped, cooked green beans

What to do:

- preheat the oven to 375 F and line muffin pans with baking cups
- in a large bowl, whisk all the dry ingredients together
- make a well in the center of the bowl and drop in the eggs, oil and 1 tbsp of salmon water
- mix well, gradually incorporating the flour into the batter, adding a little more salmon water if necessary
- when thoroughly combined, stir in the flaked salmon, green beans and ¾ cup of the cheese
- fill the baking cakes about ¾ full with batter
- bake for 15 minutes, remove and sprinkle the remaining ¼ cup of cheese on top
- return to the oven and bake an additional 5 minutes or until a toothpick inserted in the pupcakes comes out clean

*Steam or microwave in just a little water with no additives. Save the water. Let cool. *Or* you can use canned, no salt added salmon, available at health food stores or online.

Yields about 1 dozen pupcakes

Why do dogs like belly rubs?

We all know that exposing the stomach is often a submissive gesture in our pets. But our own Boo zeHound insists that his fellow canines' love of hands massaging tummies is akin to the pleasure he derives from a dogtail at the end of a long, hard day.

You Can't Lick It

What you need:

- ½ cup oat flour
- ½ cup tapioca flour
- 1 tsp baking powder
- 1 tsp baking soda
- ½ cup cheddar cheese
- 1 jar (2.5 oz) beef baby food
- 2 tbsp vegetable oil
- 1 egg
- ½ cup shredded carrots

What to do:

- preheat oven to 350 F
- line a muffin pan with baking cups
- whisk together the dry ingredients
- make a "well" in the center of the flour mix and drop in the beef, oil and egg
- gradually blend the ingredients together
- mix in the carrots and cheese
- fill the baking cups and bake for 20 minutes or 'til a toothpick inserted into a pupcake pulls out clean
- when done, let sit for a few minutes before removing to a cooling rack

Yields about 20 pupcakes

Pupcakes don't always have to be frosted to be delicious

"See this tongue? It already licked off the frosting."

At what point does a dog become old?

When you lose a dog, you lose a piece of your heart. When a new dog enters your life he fills the void with a piece of *his* heart. Perhaps, after enough dogs have filled our hearts, we will become as loving and generous as they are.

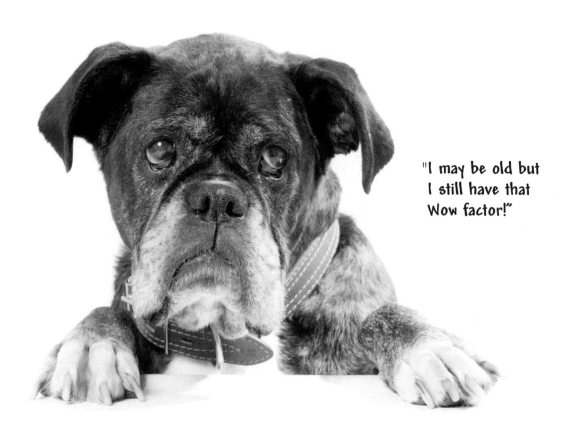

"I may be old but I still have that Wow factor!"

Bowser Wowser

What you need:

- 1 ½ cups gluten free flour
- 1 tsp baking soda
- 1 tsp baking powder
- ¼ cup flaked tuna (fresh cooked or 'no salt added' canned tuna)
- ¼ cup vegetable oil
- ½ cup low fat cottage cheese
- 1 egg
- ½ cup fresh or frozen peas

What to do:

- preheat the oven to 350 F and prepare muffin pans by lining with baking cups
- add the flour, baking powder and baking soda to a large bowl and whisk to mix
- make a well in the center of the dry mix and drop in the oil, egg and cottage cheese
- whisk together and gradually incorporate the dry ingredients into the wet mix
- stir in the tuna and peas
- drop the batter into the baking cups to ¾ full
- bake for 20 -25 minutes, 'til a toothpick inserted into a pupcake comes out clean
- cool in the pan for 2 or 3 minutes, then move to a wire rack

Yields 10 pupcakes

Upon the death of his newfoundland dog, Boatswain, in 1808, the English poet, Lord Byron, wrote a poem, "Epitaph to a Dog."

For most of us, one of the last and most beautiful things we can do for our pets is to memorialize them with a few simple words.

A favorite of The BARKtender's, by Sir William Watson is this:

His friends he loved. His fellest earthly foes--
Cats--I believe he did but feign to hate.
My hand will miss the insinuated nose,
Mine eyes that tail that wagged contempt at Fate.

MAJOR

Born a dog

Died a gentleman

"We'll go arf and arf. I'll take the top arf, you get the bottom. Fair enough?"

Sit! Stay! Eat!

What you need:

- 1 cup gluten free flour
- 1tsp baking soda
- 1 tsp baking powder
- 2 jars (2.5 oz each) chicken baby food
- ¼ - ½ cup chicken broth (recipe on page 11)
- ¼ cup vegetable oil
- 2 tbsp molasses
- ¾ cup mashed sweet potato
- 1 level tsp spirulina powder

What to do:

- preheat the oven to 350 F
- prepare a mini muffin pan with baking cups
- whisk all the dry ingredients together in a large bowl
- add the chicken, chicken broth, molasses and oil and blend into the flour mix
- stir in the sweet potato then beat the mix with a wooden spoon 'til the batter is smooth
- fill the baking cups and bake for 10 - 12 minutes or until a toothpick comes out clean from the middle of a pupcake
- cool for 3 or 4 minutes in the pan then move to a cooling rack

Don't be put off but, without frosting, this will look like something your pup ate yesterday and you just scooped up.

Puppies love this with peanut butter frosting. Find the recipe on page 104.

Yields about 24 minis

Pineapple Upside Down Pupcake

What you need:

- ½ cup brown rice flour
- ½ cup oat flour
- 1 tsp baking soda
- 2 jars (2.5 oz size) ham or chicken baby food
- ¼ cup vegetable oil
- 1 tsp vegetable oil for coating the baking cups
- unsweetened pineapple pieces, about 40
- 1 tbsp rice syrup
- 1 egg
- blueberries for garnish

What to do:

- preheat oven to 350 F
- add a very light coating of vegetable oil to the inside of *foil* baking cups then place them in a muffin pan
- in a large bowl whisk together the flour and baking soda
- blend in the baby food, vegetable oil, syrup and egg
- lay three pineapple pieces on the bottom of each baking cup
- spoon the batter into the baking cups and create a slight indentation in the top. You want the pupcakes to be fairly flat when cooked as the top will become the bottom
- bake for about 20 minutes or until a toothpick inserted in the middle of a pupcake comes out clean
- let sit for 2 or 3 minutes then move to a cooling rack
- when cool, remove the baking cups, turn the pupcakes upside down and add an extra piece of pineapple and a couple of blueberries for decoration

Yields about 10 pupcakes

Did you know...?

Pineapples grow slowly, taking up to two years to reach full size, so we pick and eat them when they are much smaller, which sometimes means they're not ripe. According to some sources, you can speed up the ripening of a pineapple by twisting off the spiky green top and standing it upside down.

A puppy can turn your world upside down and your heart
inside out

Born to sniff

It's been estimated that dogs can identify smells somewhere between 1,000 to 10,000 times better than humans. I don't know about you, but as a human I'm thankful for that when I think of some of the things dogs stick their noses into.

The Nose Knows

What you need:

- 2 ½ cups gluten-free flour
- 1 tsp baking powder
- 1 tsp baking soda
- 1 cup beef broth (see recipe on page 11)
- 1 jar (2.5 oz) beef baby food (or chicken or turkey)
- ¼ cup black molasses
- ¼ cup vegetable oil
- 2 eggs

What to do:

- preheat your oven to 350 F
- line a muffin pan with baking cups
- in a large bowl, mix the flour, baking powder and baking soda with a whisk
- make a well in the middle of the dry ingredients and add the broth, baby food, molasses, oil and eggs
- use the whisk to mix everything together, gradually incorporating the dry ingredients into the batter
- drop the batter into the baking cups
- bake for 20 - 25 minutes or until a toothpick comes out clean from the middle of a pupcake
- let the pupcakes sit in the pan for 2 or 3 minutes before moving to a wire rack to cool

Yields 12 - 14 standard pupcakes

"OMG, my nose!
I can't feel my nose!"

"Oh, Mommy! A pussycat pupcake.
Fang Q, fang Q!"

Fang Q Very Much

What you need:

- 1½ cups whole wheat flour
- ¼ cup rolled oats
- 2 tsp baking powder
- ½ tsp baking soda
- 1 tbsp dried mint (or 2 tbsp fresh chopped mint)
- ¼ cup vegetable oil
- 2 eggs
- 1 cup plain non-fat yogurt
- ½ cup 100% pure peanut butter
- 2 teaspoon rice syrup

What to do:

- preheat the oven to 350 F and prepare your muffin pans with baking cups
- whisk the dry ingredients together in a large bowl
- create a well in the center of the dry ingredients and drop in the eggs, oil, yogurt, peanut butter and rice syrup
- whisk the wet ingredients together, gradually incorporating the dry ingredients into the mix.
- stir in the mint
- fill your baking cups with the batter
- bake about 20 minutes for standard size pupcakes, 12 minutes for minis, or until a toothpick inserted in the middle of a pupcake comes out clean
- cool for 2 or 3 minutes in the pan then remove to a cooling rack

The pupcake pictured here was decorated following directions from the book, 'Hello, Cupcake!' You can recreate it using cream cheese frosting and black food dye, or use carob powder and make the cat brown.
For a more simple frosting, try the peanut butter recipe on page 104.

Yields 12 regular pupcakes and about 30 minis

Gourmutt Peanut Pupcake

What you need:

- ¾ cup oat flour
- ½ cup brown rice flour
- ¼ cup tapioca flour
- 1 tsp cinnamon
- 1 tsp baking powder
- ½ tsp baking soda
- ¼ cup 100% pure peanut butter
- ½ - ¾ cup chicken broth (recipe on page 11)
- 1 egg
- ¼ cup bacon pieces (optional)

What to do:

- preheat the oven to 350 F
- line muffin pans with baking cups
- add all the dry ingredients to a large bowl and whisk together well
- in a separate bowl, beat the egg with the peanut butter and ½ cup of chicken broth 'til completely smooth
- add the peanut butter mix to the dry ingredients and stir together thoroughly. If the mixture is too stiff add in the additional chicken broth
- stir in the bacon pieces
- pour the batter into your baking cups
- bake mini pupcakes for 10 - 12 minutes, standard pupcakes for 18 - 20 minutes, or 'til a toothpick inserted in a pupcake comes out clean
- when done, remove from the oven and let stand for a few minutes in the pan before placing cupcakes on a cooling rack
- finish with a simple cream cheese frosting (recipe on page 104)

Yields 7 or 8 regular size or 15 - 16 mini pupcakes

"Do you think these shades make me look fat?"

Some frogs and toads excrete a poison that can be very toxic - even deadly - to dogs, so keep Rover and Bella away from Jeremiah and his friends.
Signs that your pet has been in contact with a toad may be: foaming from the mouth, depression, listlessness, weakness, seizures, fever, vomiting and diarrhea.

Three Dog Pupcake

What you need:

- 8 oz ground turkey
- 1 cup canned Organic Black Beans (like Eden Foods - no salt, low fat), rinsed and drained
- 1 cup mixed lightly steamed vegetables
- 1 cup cooked organic brown rice
- ½ - 1 cup turkey or chicken broth (recipe on page 11)
- 1 egg
- 1½ cups gluten-free flour (try King Arthur or Bob's Red Mill)
- ½ cup rolled oats
- 1 tsp baking powder
- ½ tsp baking soda
- 2 tsp bone meal powder

What to do:

- preheat the oven to 350 F and prepare muffin pans by lining with baking cups
- puree the beans and vegetables with ½ cup of broth in a blender
- add the puree mix to a large bowl with the turkey, rice and egg and mix together well
- in a separate bowl, whisk together the flour, oats, baking powder, baking soda and bone meal powder
- combine the dry ingredients with the turkey mixture a little at a time. The batter will be quite stiff, so use your hands to knead it and add more broth if the batter seems too dry
- fill the baking cups
- bake for 35 - 40 minutes
- test for doneness by inserting a toothpick in the middle of a pupcake. It should come out clean
- leave the pupcakes in the pan for 2 or 3 minutes before removing to a wire rack to cool

These really need no frosting but if Danny-dog must have something, we suggest the cream cheese frosting recipe on page 104

Yields about 18 pupcakes

Gone To The Dogs

What you need:

- 1 cup rice flour
- ½ cup oat flour
- 1 tsp baking powder
- ½ tsp baking soda
- 1 jar (2.5 oz) baby food beef or chicken
- ¼ - ½ cup beef or chicken broth (recipe on page 11)
- 1 egg
- 1 cup shredded mixed vegetables*
- 1 tbsp molasses
- 1 tbsp dried parsley or 2 tbsp chopped fresh parsley (or sprinkle of spirulina powder)

What to do:

- preheat oven to 350 F and line a muffin pan with baking cups
- whisk together all the dry ingredients
- create a well in the middle of the dry ingredients and add the egg, baby food, ¼ cup of meat broth and molasses
- beat the wet ingredients together, gradually incorporating the dry mix. If need be, add the additional ¼ cup of meat broth
- stir in the shredded vegetables and parsley
- fill your baking cups and bake for 18 - 22 minutes, 'til a toothpick comes out clean from the middle of a pupcake
- let stand in the muffin pan for a few minutes before removing the pupcakes to a cooling rack

*Safe vegetables for your dog include carrot, peas, squash, green beans, asparagus, broccoli, celery, sprouts

Yields 8 - 10 pupcakes

No fair. There's nothing left for a poor puppy.

Paw prints and nose smudges on glass doors and windows break up glare and soften the light in a room

Put on the Dog

Now that you've baked your Pupcakes and shaken a Dogtail or two, it's time to gussy them up a little.

Garnishes for Dogtails

Simple garnishes:

Stirrers: Try a simple carrot or celery stick, or a green bean
Thread blueberries, small pieces of fruit or vegetables on thin rawhide* strips

Wheels: Slice cucumber, zucchini or yellow squash into rounds to put over the rim of Rover's bowl

Fruit: A ripe strawberry, slice of apple, piece of pineapple ... you get the idea

Pupsicles: Chunks of fruit or veg inserted on to rawhide* chews or carrot sticks

Meaty stuff: A single piece of jerky for dogs, a rolled-up slice or a chunk of lean, no-salt or low-salt meat, a boiled chicken liver

Herbs: Sprigs of fresh parsley or mint

Ice: Dilute vegetable juice (carrots, beetroot, broccoli or spinach) with equal parts water and freeze in fun bone or cat-shaped ice trays. You can also freeze your broth.

Stepping it up:

Carrot flower: Scrub and peel a carrot. With a channel knife, score several evenly-spaced grooves down the length of the carrot. Cut into slices. Use individual pieces or cut a small hole in the middle of each piece and thread onto a rawhide* strip.

Strawberry rose bud:
Place the strawberry stem-side down on a cutting board. Make a slice on one side to 1/8 inch from the hull. Repeat on the three other sides using the knife to ease open each "petal." Position the knife to slice a little nearer the top of the strawberry between the already cut petals. Carefully ease the slices open and you will have your rose bud.

Cucumber rose: From a cucumber, cut 10 to 14 paper thin slices at a slight angle (the pieces will be oval rather than round). Place the slices on a flat surface so they overlap each other to form a straight length. Tightly roll up the slices to form the rose and use the tip of your finger to spread the upper edges a little.

Cucumber spiral:
An English cucumber works best for this.
Cut about a 4-inch length and insert a wooden skewer through the center. Place a sharp knife at a slight angle about ¼ inch from one end of the skewered cucumber. Cut down to the skewer and continue cutting at an angle as you turn the cucumber 'til you reach the other end. Gently draw the skewer from the cucumber and you have your spiral.

*See notes on page 109

Decorating Your Pupcakes

Looks definitely are **not** everything to your dog. Let's face it, Lady and Tramp couldn't care less about your artistic abilities, they're in this for the aroma and taste. So don't sweat the pretty stuff.

Frankly, any of The BARKtender's Guide pupcakes are delicious on their own but if you want your pooch to have that little extra zing then there are only two things you really need to know...

...Low-fat cream cheese and 100% pure peanut butter.

For cream cheese frosting:

Bring the cream cheese to room temperature. Add a touch of rice syrup or low-fat plain yogurt then beat 'til light and easy to spread.

For peanut butter frosting:

Use at room temperature. Drain off any oil on the top of the peanut butter, beat together with an equal amount of low-fat cream cheese. Spread lightly on the pupcakes.

For variety:

- Color the cream cheese naturally with a little (*just* a little) carob or spirulina powder
- Add a small amount of pumpkin puree (not pie filling) to cream cheese
- Add a small amount of 100% pure applesauce to cream cheese
- Sprinkle peas or chopped/grated vegetables on cream cheese frosting, or cut vegetables into fun shapes
- Top cream cheese or peanut butter with fruit pieces
- Top with a mini dog biscuit or other treat

Cottage cheese frosting:

A quick alternative to cream cheese frosting is to use cottage cheese. Just drain some of the moisture out of the cottage cheese by putting it in a sieve over a bowl, then beat 'til smooth. Stiffen with a little bone meal powder if needed.

Decorating with Pizzazz

Here's a doggone adorable way to make Princess feel special *and* impress everyone you know by creating a **lollipup**.... and it's easier than you might think.

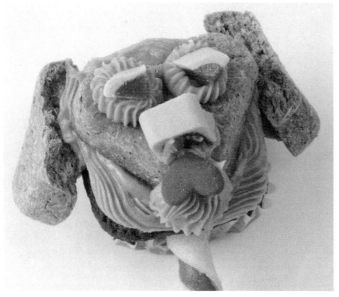

- Cover a mini pupcake with an even layer of peanut butter and cream cheese frosting
- Center a heart-shaped dog biscuit (we used *Get Naked* chicken flavor) on the top and press into the frosting
- Use a decorating bag to pipe dots of frosting on the biscuit where the eyes, nose and tongue will be
- Cut pieces of dog treats (Pur Luv Mini Bones) to finish the eyes and nose
- The tongue is a candy heart (if you're concerned about sugar in the candy, remove it before giving the lollipup)
- Take another heart-shaped biscuit and break it in half for the ears. Insert a rawhide stick or a carrot stick in the pupcake and Princess now has a Lollipup

So you're having a Pawty! It's time for something that everyone can get their teeth into.

- Add carob powder to cream cheese frosting.
- Create the body of the dog with a layer of frosted mini pupcakes then add a second layer on top, pressing the pupcakes firmly into place
- Use two pupcakes for each of the front legs, one each for the back legs and one for the tail
- Spread a layer of frosting over the front for the face
- Cut a pupcake in half and press it on to the face for the nose
- Fill a decorating bag with frosting and pipe strands over the whole dog to create a shaggy look, leaving the face untouched except for the nose (You may need to stiffen the frosting up by adding a small amount of flour. Go easy, though, you don't want to taste the flour)
- Pipe circles of plain cream cheese frosting for the eyes and add dog treats to the middle
- Chill, then mold frosting for the ears
- Candy has been used for the tongue and bow for decoration only. Remove these before giving to your pet.

Feeding No-Nos

Which of us doesn't love to give our friends the occasional treat? Unfortunately, good intentions can have deadly consequences. That's why we've been so careful with the ingredients in The BARKtender's Guide recipes. And in case you think of slipping poochie a little something from the kitchen table, remember that not all people foods are safe for dogs.

If you ever think that your pet may have ingested a potentially poisonous substance, call the **ASPCA Animal Poison Control Center: (888) 426-4435** or your local veterinarian.

Definite No-Nos

Alcohol
Giving alcohol to your pet not only puts Rover in serious potential harm, it shows you to be a complete moron. Even small amounts of alcohol can cause vomiting, diarrhea, central nervous system dysfunction, breathing difficulties and, yes, death.

Avocado
Maybe you like guacamole but don't let your chihuahua near it. Every part of the avocado, including the bark, contains persin, which can cause vomiting and diarrhea.

Caffeine
That morning jolt is poison for a pooch. Signs of caffeine poisoning are vomiting, diarrhea, tremors, panting, excessive thirst, rapid heart rate, seizures and, again, death. Remember, too, caffeine is found in many sodas, some teas and most stimulant drinks.

Chocolate
We absolutely understand the appeal of chocolate.... for people, but sharing it with your BFF can be killer! Chocolate contains both caffeine *and* theobromine, which have similar effects on Fido - vomiting, diarrhea, abnormal heart rhythm, thirst, seizures and death. The darker the chocolate, the higher the content of these toxic substances.

Grapes and Raisins
Although a number of fruits are safe and healthy treats, grapes are definitely not one of them. Just a few grapes or raisins can cause illness, potentially leading to kidney failure and death. It's not known what substance in grapes causes such toxicity but keep them out of your pet's reach.

Macadamia nuts
These can cause serious symptoms of weakness, paralysis, tremors, vomiting and rapid heart rate that can lead to fatality.

Yeast dough
The problem with yeast dough is that it can rise in your pup's stomach. This can stretch the abdomen, causing considerable pain and can actually lead to rupture of the stomach or intestines. Additionally, as the yeast ferments it produces alcohol that can bring about alcohol poisoning.

Xylitol and other artificial sweeteners
Used as a sweetener in many products - candy, gum, diet foods, toothpaste - it can cause an increase in insulin, which may lead to vomiting, lethargy, loss of coordination, seizures and eventual liver failure in just a few days.

Bacon and hot dogs

Cured meats generally contain nitrates, which can be toxic, causing abdominal pain, diarrhea or convulsions. There are nitrate-free varieties available but use with caution and check with your vet.

Milk and cheese

There's a school of thought that cow's milk should only be for calves. It's certainly not for dogs, other than in occasional small portions. Canines lack a significant amount of lactase, necessary to break down lactose in milk and so are likely to suffer diarrhea, other digestive problems and allergies. Yogurt, although a dairy product, is generally considered safe provided you pick one that has live active bacteria and no sugars or artificial sweeteners.

Onions and Garlic

Some people consider garlic to be a beneficial additive to Muffin's diet. It's quite commonly an ingredient in commercial dog foods. However, dogs that eat onion and garlic in all forms - raw, cooked, powdered - are in danger of anemia. Small amounts on occasion may be acceptable but signs of red blood cell toxicity are listlessness, breathing difficulty, vomiting.

Peaches, Persimmons and Plums

It's the pits from these fruits that are a problem. Persimmon seeds can cause inflammation of the small intestines; peach and plum pits contain cyanide.

Rawhide and Pig Ears

What can we say but "chewse" with care. Yes, some of The BARKtender's Guide recipes include rawhide as part of a garnish however, here's what you need to know. Some imported rawhide *may* contain toxins such as arsenic, lead, formaldehyde, mercury and others. Salmonella poisoning has been reported from ingesting tainted rawhide. The chews can get stuck in the esophagus, stomach or intestines, requiring surgical removal and potentially killing your pet. So, always monitor your pet's chewing and if in doubt about giving rawhide, find an alternative or omit the garnish.

Salt

So you like a few salty chips with your cocktail. Duke doesn't need any with his dogtail. Too much salt may induce vomiting, diarrhea, tremors, elevated temperature or worse.

Sugar

As with people, too much can contribute to obesity, dental problems and possibly diabetes. At The BARKtender's Guide we favor lower glycemic rice syrup or blackstrap molasses.

- The raw pet food movement has gained a lot of traction in recent years. The BARKtender neither endorses nor disagrees with this diet but urges that you talk with your veterinarian before making any dietary changes.

- You will see that we have used raw egg in a couple of our dogtail recipes but stress that only the freshest, organic eggs be included to avoid potential food poisoning. If in any doubt at all about the quality of the eggs or Fluffy's ability to digest them, omit them from the recipe. It will still taste delicious.

- About bone meal. Be sure to buy bone meal that is intended for human and animal consumption. Do NOT buy from the home and garden section; this bone meal contains fertilizer and will poison your pet.

- About gluten-free. As with people, it's not uncommon for dogs to be gluten intolerant, which is why The BARKtender likes to bake with gluten-free flours such as oat, rice and tapioca. Several companies also make gluten-free blends (King Arthur and Bob's Red Mill among others); just make sure the product is labeled "certified gluten-free."

- Baby foods can be useful in recipes rather than having to puree your own meats, fruits and veg. Organic, of course, is best. Check labels on all brands; some contain lemon juice or citric acid, which can cause stomach upset, though rarely in these trace amounts.

- Fat can contribute to pancreatitis in dogs. In its acute form, your pal can go into shock within hours and die. So, if you've been wondering why our recipes are made with only low-fat products, now you know.

"I shouldn't have had all those pupcakes before dinner"

The Tasting Team

Before gaining space in The BARKtender's Guide every recipe had to be tested and given a "paws up" by our tasting team. This prestigious panel of "taste buds" comprises some of the finest noses and connoisseurs of kibble in the business.
Allow us to introduce them.

Angel. You've already met Angel on the inside cover of *The BARKtender's Guide*. At about 8 months of age, close to death from starvation and with broken bones from severe beatings, she was rescued by Southern Hope Humane Society (southernhopehumane.com). She was in an outside pen with no shelter, surviving on twigs and leaves and her own feces.

Now-a-days, six year old Angel is a beautiful, happy girl who just loves squeaky toys and squirrel chasing. Her preferred dogtail is the *Angel's Kiss* (of course), with its smooth texture and subtle blend of peanut and carob, and she's partial to a *Slow Comfortable Sniff*, another peanut butter delight.

For pupcakes, Angel is particularly partial to the *Bowser Wowser* and *The Nose Knows*, both gluten-free and low fat, essential for her sensitive digestive system.

Vinny is Angel's self-appointed guardian. They met at Southern Hope and Angel has been his girl ever since. Of uncertain pedigree the 11-year old sports an air of cocky, untamed masculinity, and is considered to be quite the mutt-magnet. He also tends to think that any lap is an open invitation.

Not surprisingly, he enjoys a little *Angel's Kiss* and occasional *Sex in the Dog Park*. But at the end of a hard day there's nothing better than a *Dirty Muttini*, a lift-your-leg, dangerous to both sexes drink that suits his personality.

The rich combination of chicken, peanut butter and cinnamon in the *Gourmutt Peanut pupcake* definitely causes Vinny to salivate. And as with Angel, he finds the beefy base of *The Nose Knows* to be irresistible, while *Droolin' on a Sunday Afternoon* is another favorite.

Coco has never met a dogtail or pupcake she didn't love. A puppy mill rescue, six yearl old Coco, spent the first few years of her life stacked in a filthy crate being used as a birthing machine. She was completely unschooled in house training, stair climbing, even running but has tackled all obstacles with determination and has achieved unparalleled success.

She brings the same enthusiasm, if rather lacking in discrimination, to her taste-testing duties. Her absolute favorite dogtail, by just a lick, is the *Angel's Kiss*, closely followed by a *Slow Comfortable Sniff*, *Lappletini*, *Fuzzy Navel* and *Howling Banana Banshee*. When it comes to pupcakes, Coco is an equal opportunity eater and will gladly chow down on *Pawty Animal pupcakes*, *Droolin' on a Sunday Afternoon* or any other pupcake around.

Lucy is a high energy Super Mutt. At just two years of age she is the youngest of the team with an endlessly optimistic personality.

Adopted when she was seven months old, Lucy doesn't have a mean bone in her body. She loves all people and pets alike and lives to play.

The *Lappletini*, with its notes of crisp apple and rich turkey broth is Lucy's favorite muttini along with another turkey-based drink, the *Dogmopolitan*.

For pupcakes, as you might expect, she's a *Pawty Animal* girl, favoring the sweet watermelon taste and surprise, surprise! she also really enjoys turkey in her pupcakes and ranks the *Give a Dog a Bone* pupcakes with its blend of cottage cheese, turkey and molasses as one of her top choices.

Domino is a stately 15-year old and the most critical of our tasters. His mom adopted him from a border collie rescue but became suspect of his breeding when he exhibited none of their traits. A DNA test revealed him to be Labrador, Chow and German Shepherd. He has a great sense of humor and a tendency to goose mom if she's a little slow getting the leash out.

Of the dogtails, Domino's top pick is the *Dogmopolitan*. He likes the earthy notes of pork and turkey and the silky texture that cream cheese gives the drink.

For pupcakes his tastes definitely lean towards the richer, cheesey varieties. He salivates for the apple, cheddar, molasses combination of the *Tres Licks Pupcakes*, and the melding of hearty cheese, beef and carrot in the *You Can't Lick It* pupcakes.

George was rescued only hours before he was due to be euthanized. A four-year old border collie beagle mix of unknown background, he has struggled with biting issues. After twice being returned from potential homes his mom decided to keep him and work with him. Two years later he is a different dog and a happy member of his loving family.

George, along with Lucy, gives the *Lappletini* his highest rating for its well-balanced blend of turkey, apple and cheese.

His favorite pupcake is *You Can't Lick It*, closely followed by *Woof It Down*, another cheese and apple combination, moistened with yogurt and a hint of rice syrup. He also joins Domino in his assessment of the *Tres Licks Pupcakes*.

Suzy, at 17 years old, is the grand dame of the team. Another rescue, of course, she's been with her mom, Robin Taylor of Gwinnett Pet Watchers in Georgia, since she was 7 months old.

A full-bred border collie, Suzy is super smart and in her younger days could boast a vocabulary of more than 50 words that she understood. Unfortunately, she now suffers from hearing problems that make her a little unstable, for which her family playfully call her Psycho Suzy.

When it comes to dogtails, Suzy's preference is for a meaty broth with a smooth blend of cheese. Her number one pick of the pupcakes is *Fang Q Very Much*, with its rich mix of oats, yogurt and peanut butter. She's also a fan of the *Gourmutt Peanut Pupcake*, a gluten-free delight of peanut butter and chicken with a hint of cinnamon.

Jake is another youngster at three. Until he was lucky enough to be taken in by his paw parent life must have been miserable for this handsome australian shepherd. He was tossed out of a car at a rest area, in bad shape and with cigarette burns over his body. Happily, a kindly truck driver picked him up.

It was intended that Jake spend just a night at his mom's house while more permanent arrangements were made but he won her over by putting his paws on her shoulders and resting his forehead against her's.

The Dogmopolitan is Jake's preferred potion. As for pupcakes, there's nothing he doesn't like. His absolute favorites, however, are You Can't Lick It and the Pound Pupcake, made of chicken mixed with carrots, peas, a little cooked egg and parsley.

Here's to wet noses and wagging tails!

Index

What do you get when you cross a bulldog with a shih tzu?

Bullshitz!